T0149250

The
FOUND
LOVE

MICHEL CAZAL

WESTBOW
P R E S S®
A DIVISION OF THOMAS NELSON
& ZONDERVAN

WestBow Press books may be ordered through booksellers or by contacting:

WestBow Press
A Division of Thomas Nelson & Zondervan
1663 Liberty Drive
Bloomington, IN 47403
www.westbowpress.com
1 (866) 928-1240

Because of the dynamic nature of the Internet, any web addresses or links contained in this book may have changed since publication and may no longer be valid. The views expressed in this work are solely those of the author and do not necessarily reflect the views of the publisher, and the publisher hereby disclaims any responsibility for them.

Any people depicted in stock imagery provided by Thinkstock are models, and such images are being used for illustrative purposes only. Certain stock imagery © Thinkstock.

ISBN: 978-1-5127-2747-0 (sc)
ISBN: 978-1-5127-2748-7 (hc)
ISBN: 978-1-5127-2746-3 (e)

Library of Congress Control Number: 2016900961

Print information available on the last page.

WestBow Press rev. date: 1/27/2016

To the princess of life,
the sons of love,
and the lovely daughter.

In the midst of the shouts of the crowd die our hearts to the desire to be alive—the desire and the envy.

The hour. The hour of the first step, of the child learning to walk. The hour to wake up. Another life ahead, waiting for us. The real life. Walk as since time immemorial, where love fills the unformed and void universe. Silent, seated, he waits.

Love, true love. One who gives himself, who does not count himself, who cannot be deserved, and who is by himself in absolute freedom. Whoever starts when everything has ended. He who makes life in a new present, who hunts the past to prepare a future full of hope. For that, abandon everything, surrendering ourselves until we feel loved, until we know be loved: the heart open, ready to receive.

Love is the starting point of all things, the origin. And there was light, since the beginning.

Love knows. He knows that he is the essence of life.

Love has created the world. This is an unknown kind of matter. Love extends and stretches itself in the universe, and the universe founds love in its infinite dimension and depth. Love is substance, evidence. Love reigns in its kingdom. It cannot be owned. We belong to it. It bears us. It carries us. It is the door through which we enter into and then emerge from the hidden but real life, the ignored but eternal life.

Receive everything like a gift. The true rest.

Doing nothing. Receiving before he who is. The lightest, the fairest, position. An endless resource. The power of a manifested love in the capacity of unlimited gift.

I own because I have received.

I shall reach the edge. There is a river flowing. There is a path that goes up to heaven. It leads to the palace of a fantastic world. I shall walk on it, lay my feet on, rest my head, and drop my thoughts for the bloom and the effusion of life, of an enchanting spirit. My heart is transposed, changed with the brightness of a gushing light, which enlightens my spirit with the endless joy of a found love.

I celebrate every day,
The arrival of the day,
By singing a hymn to love.

The thought of eternity
Makes me king
This morning.

Alone I came unto you.
Again I came toward you.
I desire to fully belong to you.

My soul touched,
I am at your feet,
Seeking in my thoughts.

My life now belongs to you.
I seek refuge in your love
Every morning.

This morning I am removing my shoes from my feet to stand on the Holy Land. I have received a treasure. It was entrusted to me. I have to share it, to give it. This treasure is light. This treasure is power. This treasure is freedom from chains of ignorance, darkness. This treasure is life of the spirit reconciled in the flesh, in a changed heart, in a heart watered by a new flow.

This light grows up and spreads out its rays, extends its brightness on the banks of intelligence, on the banks of the heart of being. It travels a path sown with precious stones, in the midst of a luxuriant and abundant nature drained by the tumultuous waters of the source of life, leading at their bend to oases of joy and peace where grow the flowers of happiness, where love gives itself from hand to hand. I would like for that love to be poured into the hearts of all people of this land, for love saves the world.

To raise my voice and shout my joy. To serve on this mountain in the land flowing with milk and honey.

I never left the land where I was born. Everything takes me back there.

I am walking on the way back, the one that brought me back to you. Our hearts are pulled with ropes of love.

I have known true love. Now I can leave the earth, because heaven is open to me.

It is wonderful to have this heaven opened and to see the sunshine.

Much time has gone by.
On this path have I walked.
I know not anymore if in my heart
What I have seen is happiness.

Love
Is very far away.
You look for it.
It took another way
To live another fate.

One day blooms life again.
Nothing can stop it.
In paradise, children laugh,
No more worry.
It is wonderful.

Peace
Is in our heart,
Is our true light.
He is the light.

I learned by loving. I learned by surrendering myself. I learned by walking as a child.

We must grow up like children, grow up to become as children.

To everything there is a season. It takes time for the child to grow up and become an adult. The same goes for the right thought to develop and manifest by itself in what it is. To believe, admit, and accept without doubt, unfailingly, that everything is possible. This possibility must proceed from itself. Everything is possible if we are on the way, holding this right, strong, powerful, sincere thought that everything is always possible.

In paradise, children laugh. If we have to wake up early, demonstrate an inflexible will, be animated by an undying desire to seek, maintain, take care of, and protect this thought; if we must devote time, invest all that we have, give up ourselves to taste its presence, its power, often at the expense of all other things, of our own life; if the world has to be reversed, and if we have to come close to folly, we can be sure that in return, everything will be given to the one who makes of it the unique purpose of his thoughts, to he who has desired to be like it, to welcome it within himself, to conform to it.

My beloved,
Come beside me.
I shall give you
All you desire,
Shall water your soul,
The source of
All beautiful thoughts,
Shall blow in your heart
The wind of
All beautiful words,

The color
Of time.

My beloved,
Stay close to me
Lest your foot
Hit against a stone
To move forward on
The land of your destiny,
To find again
Outside
Life of other kind,

The color
Of time.

The tears you have shed
Are on your mind like the dew;
The dreams you have shaped,
They are true.

You will see before your eyes
All you have imagined,
A present from God.

You take my hand,
And things are not the same.
You lead me up to your heart.
I can rejoice at the sound of your name
Now I am sure that it's true.

I know that they will be many
To take my hand,
And we shall follow the path,
Our hearts satiated with tomorrows
That will never end.

Finally, I hold her hand. I am no longer alone. We can run now; our hearts are light. My sweetheart, my daughter, my beloved, why have you not told me that your heart was broken, that your soul was upset? I am here, I am here, and I stretch out my hand to you. Do not be afraid. Have no fear. Life belongs to us. This is our destiny, the one that suits us.

Why do you think that I have been looking for you all this time? It is because I was waiting for you. It is because I knew you were there. Every word, every thought, every breath led me to you. I shall never forsake you.

I tied up myself to you,
To your soul and your life,
Without asking you anything
But what you are able to give:
A moment of eternity.

Our hearts were filled.
Our hands were united.
Our lips were found,
A moment reconciled.

Don't be afraid.
Don't look behind.
The past
Has gone away.

Don't cry anymore.
Open your eyes.
Life for you
Has started over.

The water of the river
Flows unto the sea.
If you are afraid,
Pray.

Death was not stronger than life.
The earth was opened.
The heavens split.
That which was bitter
Became like honey.

Now wake up.
He's calling you.
Listen to his words.
They are true.
You see, your soul
Will be in peace.

Today he shines
Like the sun.
His heart of love
Is forever.
By his Spirit
He gives life.

All your past
Will be forgotten.
Nothing
Will stop you.
In liberty
Will you sing.

Love is made of gift, forgiveness, and surrender.
He is our true nature.
Without him we are nothing.
By him we become what we are.

With him all things belong to us,
The visible and invisible.
United to the essential,
We reach heaven.

Love is the smallest seed,
The fragile plant that supports our lives.
But it produces the tree of many fruits
Whose roots dive into the source of life.

Love is the smooth breeze that lifts up our souls,
The song that wakes he who slumbers,
The fire that tests the gold of our hearts,
The light that opens our eyes.

The poor becomes rich;
The rich, humble;
The fool, intelligent;
The wise, a child.

Never thinking,
Without ceasing,
Opening for us the door
Of eternity.

We have trampled love under the steps of our doubts. Proud and assured, we ignored him, holed up in the fortress of our hearts, dragooned behind the walls of our thoughts. We were bathed in the sad waters of our tears. We awaited deliverance. We expected love. But when he came, we did not recognize him.

But he comes. He still comes. He always comes. He runs, hastening. He flies over the seas. He crosses the mountains. He covers like a bolt of lightning the distance that divides our hearts. There he lays out again the dew of heaven, the purifying oil, the vivifying scent. Then the sea of our hearts soothes itself. Our soul becomes like the one of the weaned child. We sleep peacefully. We drink each day from a fresh stream of water—the pure water, the true treasure. This water is like the dew of heaven, and we shall gather it every morning in the palms of our hands before the heat of the day makes it disappear, before the ardor of the sun takes it away from our eyes. One drop of this water makes fertile the vast expanse of our hearts.

We know now, because we have tasted. We are loved. Our life is precious. We are born, carried to the land of freedom. So it was true, what the true witnesses had told us. Let's climb on the mountain; let's contemplate the extent of happiness; let's scrutinize the distant horizon of our hearts. We are alive!

The Promised Land. We see it in the distance, but we do not know the way. Let us open our hearts. There is the door of eternity. Love is the key that opens the door of our hearts. We enter into, and we go out of, the heart of eternity.

Love is the way. He makes us hear a living word to learn, understand. Everything is new. We are living in the permanent and constant renewal of love, refreshed by the possibility of new things.

The path of life is the one that leads to heaven. Let there the thoughts of love rise up to heaven, and join the symphony of the angels and the ball of the stars.

Love is the found path under my feet upon which I have walked to become a man, to become a perfect and accomplished man. I move forward since this is my destiny. I have been called to walk in the light, to walk in this light, which has created all things, which reveals his own heart to humanity so that we may hear wonderful things, believing that everything is possible and seeing the beauty of life wherever it lies.

I have tasted what is true and gracious. It remains in me an everlasting flavor, the sap of life. My life is an open book whose pages are written day by day, because I am running.

I was called to be, to be in all plenitude. Radiate. Shine. Come out like the new day.

I learned to be, to exist. This is my struggle for life. So yes, I am. And that is sufficient for me. May it be so for all those who are blessed. Let them acknowledge that to love is to exist and that to live is to love.

Now I know that everywhere, I am, anytime.

We are moving constantly toward what we are, and this is largely because we have been and we have already lived it. Our life on earth is a time of grace and blessing, so that we love.

Love is the Redeemer.
It enlightens our hearts.
It is your light
That shines on us
When you flood us
With your love.

Love. Welcome. Accept. The treasures of life flock, happy to find a land, a place to rest. The wealth itself, the body too, weary of seeing people exalting and seeking them with much greed and covetousness, are delighted to find souls able to appreciate those treasures, in righteousness.

The blessing is a song of joy, an ode to life on earth. We love when we bless. It opens the door to abundant joy. Let us go into the world. Let us run into the career with blessing and grace in mind and heart. We would be rich if we blessed, if our time and intelligence were devoted to giving blessings. We would be in a permanent celebration.

Man bears in himself the weight of his gladness and the joy of his freedom.

Happiness is the path to reach what we hope for and to achieve what we believe in. This is not the result. Since we see it, can we still hope for it? But we must always love it.

Let there be no obstacle to love, a permanent welcome in our hearts.

Open your heart and you will see happiness.
You will see love coming into your life
Like a river of living water.
He will surprise you.
You will no longer fear.
He will show you high ways,
Paths on which your foot has not walked.
He will make you climb above steep hills
To make you contemplate
A forgotten country.

There you will find
Joy, rest, freedom.
Your eyes will be delighted
By a thousand wonders.
You will see your beloved
Appearing like the sun.
He will rise.
He will take your hand.
He will tell you,
"Come, let's go by the way."

He will kiss your feet.
You will have a taste of
The dew of his lips.
You will sleep beside him
In an endless desire.

He will enchant your soul
By the beauty of his hands.
You will be his, your beloved.
He will be yours, his love found.

Thirsty. My spirit dry. I believed I had reached sure places to find refuge from a tormented life, a broken heart, a doubtful mind. Again, this was but the sad reality of a continual illusion. I shouted to the infinite, "Come, show me the way!" Light has sprung in darkness. Peace has overflowed my heart.

I came out. I opened my eyes on an unknown land, a far country, one that my soul had never seen. I said, "You are here," to the one who watched on me. "Thus, it was you who attracted me." I awoke after an endless night.

I look at the sea.
I lift up my eyes.
I seek in the universe
If there is a sun
Which is different,
An everlasting romance.

Here I am
Without speaking,
Without crying,
Without running,
Singing *maloya*.

Life is not so much a mystery.
If you dig deep in the ground,
You will find joy and happiness,
The scent of a good flower.

Here you are
Without speaking,
Without crying,
Without running,
Singing maloya.

I knew a grace that descends from above and opens the gates of heaven, feeding me, establishing me in things that belong to me. My heart glows with the only spark of that light. My soul is animated by the breath of the spirit. My flesh trembles under the waves of the river of life.

Love is a devouring fire that melts our hearts in the crucible of the most tried and proven gold to truly reveal who we are. I hear men and women shouting and crying in pain because love has gone away, far out of their life. But he comes, if only we would stretch out our hands.

The reversal of thought. The upheaval of hearts. Things one has neither seen nor heard, not ever.

Your look is sufficient. Your thought imposes itself, as it is so much strong.

He remained alone, forsaken, in complete darkness. This is the work of sacrifice, the way of love, the path of righteousness. Abandon oneself. Do you only want to receive, take from me, take me with you, bear me in your heart, and cherish me as a newborn child, the object of all attention? We must learn to walk like men who received peace, as enlightened men. He makes me walk in ignored countries, in unexpected lands where everything becomes light, even the most heavy burden, for there lies freedom. Then I sing. I sing because I live.

Limitless. To become oneself, to get free.

There is no true love without freedom. Truth sets us free. Grace gives us love sharing.

We must dig, dig with our lamps burning. Not to do it in the darkness of our lives is to risk losing ourselves. One does not get lost on the path of truth, for it leads to love.

Love made flesh. Truth and grace. The spirit in the flesh. The language of the heart. The pearl of high value. For where your treasure is, there will your heart be also.

Love is strong. Love gives life, true life. Life to the full, manifested, like a source flowing in our heart and refreshing the soul. The burning desire to know, heated by the fire of passion. To know the fulfillment, filled with this power of love that leads, reassures, enriches. Abandon everything to him. Surrender all to believe in the best, to receive his presence. Believe that all things are possible even when the sky is darkened. Go beyond the veil to reach the wonderful. Open our hearts so that love reaches us.

Stand fast in the thought of love. May that thought dwell continuously deep in our hearts so that they are strengthened. "You will keep in perfect peace those whose minds are steadfast, because they trust in you."

Caught in the prison of our hearts, deprived of liberty. Remaining outside is like being imprisoned. Being inside is having found life, entering into it, having returned back to the source, to the origin. Stop turning around unceasingly like one trapped in a whirling without ever understanding, without ever reaching the truth.

Make room in your heart for what is new. Welcome what is unknown to you. Let your steps be led, fed, by love.

The unison of the hearts in love. The resonance of the vibration. Make it the subject of research. Seek truth, not knowledge, to be able to love.

Love leads to the gift of oneself. Love is the engine of the gift. The true justice is the one that reconciles duty and love. Love leads to the gift, which itself leads to grace, to freedom. When we are free, we truly are. Love leads to the truth. We live. The one who loves, live. Let us love, and we shall accomplish what is right, slightly, freely.

Replace justice with love. Never look behind, though the heart resolutely turns toward the future, with passion.

Love is the bread of life, the bread that feeds the soul and fills the spirit. It makes us victorious over everything. It makes us reign.

Our heart is made for love. Our heart is our inner being. If we desire that love enter into it, we must open the door. Make room for him so that he settles down in our lives, so that he lives with us, within us.

From where does it come that love moves away from us? Love runs away, turns his back to us, and leaves when he does not find his place anymore. He leaves. He departs from our heart when we put him out and close the door. This happens because of the wounds of our heart. The unhealed wounds of the heart slowly distill the poison of resentment, bitterness, and hard feelings into our suffering soul. The poison of our soul. Forgiveness runs away, and love follows him. Our heart dries up. It becomes like a barren land, a desert, a hostile land wherein it is then impossible for love to bloom. Instead the thorns grow up. A ruin. Love cannot resist the heat of the sun. We are left alone. We languish. But deep inside us, hope never flies away. The thirst grips us. We have this hope that the desert will green again, that love will bloom again. For love never dies.

Love is patient. He forgives all things, he believes all things, he hopes all things. We shall then have left the dryness of our heart to enter into the land flowing with milk and honey, the blessed land of life.

As long as we shall try to approach love with understanding, he will run away from us, for love is a cry, a breath, a burning desire.

Open the eyes of my heart
That the truth may enter into it
Like a river of living water.

I love you above all things.

You did stop the tumult that was in my heart.

All the treasures of heaven
That I keep with me,
All eternal treasures
That I bear within me.
You came to pick me.
I do not forget
Who called me.
I did not know you.

I am nothing,
A shooting star,
A burst of light.

This is what I am
Before you this morning.
I lift my hands.

You stretch the limits of the country.
You stretch it farther away from
The shores of my destiny.

You, an enlightened beggar,
Have enriched my life.

The beauty of things. Love life. See the world in all its beauty and reality. We contemplate it as something that comes from elsewhere, like something that fills all with its presence.

The beauty of things enchants me, like a river that carries me and leads me to the source of life. Go searching for beauty where she dwells, the hidden treasure, buried in our souls. To be driven, carried by the stream of the spirit.

Develop the ability to love, because on it depends our salvation. The accession of the heart is inconceivable to him whose heart is closed, to him whose heart has not given up itself.

There is only one reign, the one of love. There is only one kingdom, the one of unity. There is only one King, the One who is forever.

Except the grain of wheat falls into the ground and dies, it abides alone; but if it dies, it brings forth much fruit.

Love is established on certainties, even maybe one only, that of the assurance to find again what has been given. Like a seed that brings forth fruit, attending to the growth of what was at the very beginning a small reality and according to the power that works in it, it becomes the most abundant tree, the most exuberant source in a magnificence conducive to joy, to the exaltation of the eternal reality of life—the found life, the enlightened path, the purified desire, the granted wish. Reality as a refuge: the happiness of having found.

Strong as the lion, meek as the lamb. Love in the spirit is a fire, a fire that consumes us, body, soul and mind, in the reality of being, in the eternity of life. Our hearts burn in the flames of this living love, are warmed by his presence, are lifted up by his power.

It took power to open the doors of heaven. They were moved.

Love is seated
In the midst of the garden of a thousand flowers
Bearing the brightness of every color,
The fragrance of all scents,
The honey of all tastes.

Love shines with brightness
Like a child
Who sees the world
With joy,
At each step
Finding a treasure
Without knowing
That it is gold.

Love is like a devouring fire
That kindles the heart.
Love is like the dew of heaven
That shines in the sun.
Love is like a land
Seeded with all blessings.
Love is like a smooth breeze
That caresses time.

Would there be a reality other than love, an eternity other than the one provided by love, a truth other than the one demonstrated by love?

One has to give the purest love. It reveals itself only by touching the truth. We have lost the substance of truth, which is love.

Hearts meet up only in love.

Love is above all things.

I am not ashamed of your love. It is the power from heaven given for salvation.

My heart is the garden of your love.

"There is no one righteous, not even one."

There is a righteousness that comes from works and that finds its justification in accomplishment. The righteousness, which seeks to reach perfection, always elusive and distant. This is not the way of love. It is the way of power, strength, and tyranny. The way, which converts the abandon, the original and founding loneliness, in a manner of living.

Which force? If it exists, it is an illusion, a might coming only from the flesh. We must stop living in fallacy and lies, which lock us in an unreal world of illusion.

The inner force in humankind brings forth frustration. It may be the strength to survive, but surely it is not a source of life.

The world is upset. Soon, we shall fight for a drop of water, a word of truth, a moment of love. This is what awaits us. The bread will be removed from us, the path closed. Hearts will be desperate because there will not be a single hope of life and freedom. Then we shall know that life is more than food.

We are living in the time when people lift up their heads, when soon people will come out from oppression, all the captives, all those in chains, all those in exile, all those detained without cause, unjustly, whose only desire is to live, to be free, to rejoice, to participate in the feast and in the celebration, the song of hope.

I fought battles and won victories with the armed wing of my intelligence, victories credited to my reputation and power. But deep inside, I cry. Sadness and distress infect me like leprosy. Who knows my trouble? I am like the Syrian general, a winner outside but defeated inside, forced to hide under the mantle so that others do not see the work of sickness, the open wound, my weakness.

Where are the waters of the Jordan into which I can plunge and be purified so that my soul comes out washed of its uncleanness and my heart healed from its wounds? Where are these waters?

I am weak. Toughness is a mask that I put on to hide my weakness. But I am not this wound; I am not this leprosy that bonds my flesh and breaks it up. I do not want to bear this illness—like the funerary mark of my life, like an open grave in my heart—anymore.

It is not the spirit of freedom. It is a kind of sterile and sickly downfall of the human being, an infirmity of thought that distorts reality, cuts one off from truth, and deprives one of liberty.

"I will praise you, for I am fearfully and wonderfully made." This is the truth. The river of life is a quiet one, a peaceful and quiet river that flows into the ocean of eternity. But our false thoughts, our unjust feelings, turn it away from its riverbed, devastating everything in its way, leaving behind a path of destruction.

It is a desperate fight, an unceasing headlong rush, entangled in a marsh of bad days and outdated works. Change that, this inner destructive and murderous conception, even before I consider my name as a wound, as a shameful thing to hide.

This abasement of body, soul, and mind: it prevents me from reaching perfection, a perfection that I believed I could reach, with illusion. But it was based on a mere intellectual understanding of things, of truth.

The voice that leads us always seems to be the one of judgment, judgment of self and of others, and always makes us stay on a path of failure and deception, bearing regret. This is not the voice of love.

We must break down resistance, this tyrannical voice of accusation that endlessly requires us to being perfect, to reach perfection. Why? What is there to prove? What is sought to redeem? Why carry guilt? Victimization leads to guilt. This is not the way of love.

A distorted love that is always looking to place one above the other is definitely not love.

Love entails no settling of scores, no miserly accounts of alleged mutual debts that we would hold, one to another. This is not love but accounting, which brings resentment, regrets, disenchantment.

Judgment prevents any demonstration of compassion. One has to keep silent before suffering. How much pain has been inflicted on others because of our own misery!

I do not want any message of condemnation. I need protection. Man judges only by appearance, not according to what lies in the heart. So we judge, we condemn, in the name of morality, of our religious piety, and of our justice, which reveals itself to be unjust. But how many wounds are we carrying deep inside our heart that prevent us from being free and from wholly following the way of righteousness, that make us fallen beings of our own identity, that cut us off from what we really are? We must thus stop judging and condemning. Give up this feeling of guilt that persists in defiling the heart.

Like a blind man in the middle of the day groping, searching for his way, the path, I lived caught in a prison. Like a lion in a cage, like a raging dog, I was under the law, the terror of perpetual indebtedness, living a prison in which I tried to have others incarcerated.

I acted like the servant who had received a single talent and then buried it in the ground, who hid it in fear of not being able to multiply it and then to render to his master, to present to his prescriber, what he had received in payment, the outcome of his labor. I too hid myself. I razed the walls. I did as if I were not, as if I received nothing, as if I were good for nothing. I did consider myself not worthy to receive, because I wrongly believed that the reward was coming from me.

I was like the faithless people, again and always wandering in the desert, unable to cross the border separating them from the Promised Land, a land flowing with milk and honey, people caught in dissatisfaction, rebellion, and bitterness. Murmurings and threats they voiced against the entire world, against God, against life. These people, because of their own foolishness, of their detention, of their stubbornness eventually destined for perdition, destruction, and slow death, without their having tasted the promises, known happiness, or taken part in the celebration.

I desired love. I do not really know what love and grace are.

The balance between power and wisdom is love.

Love is for the strong.

"Surely goodness and mercy shall follow me all the days of my life."

Life is always like that. One thing ends. Another begins.

Time does not exist. Change is the most important thing, powerful and triumphant change. Things can change. They are changing.

We need a spiritual strength based on love and the knowledge of the truth to lift us from falsehood, from the folly of illusion, and to make all things possible.

All things are possible. To be no longer indebted. We do not owe anything to one another but love. Love finally. Yes, everything is possible.

We need to be loved, to be freed from the heaviness of guilt, to be unloaded from judgment. We do not need to be judged. We need to be loved.

We are made for love, not to be thinking machines.

Suffering is not the destiny of humankind. Restriction, failure, is not a fate. The true destiny of humankind is to reign.

Striking the coup de grâce. Live another life before it is too late, as my destiny disappears with time. I know that I can be. Soon I shall. I say it as of today: I am!

May my life know a new day, the accomplishment of myself.

Open the door! "They will go out and find green pastures."

May joy, grace, peace, happiness, love, and light come! "For you shall go out with joy. And be led with peace."

To be touched by grace, this is what avails anything. This is the issue of life, of faith, of freedom, of love. Maybe grace has not reached yet all the nooks and crannies of my soul and of my heart.

"It is not good for man to be alone." The purpose of creation is to unite, to reunite. Take hold of this stretched hand beyond time and space, this touching hand, this blessing hand, the caressing hand of he who is meek and lowly of heart.

Life is precious; happiness is real. Happiness is a devotion. One must have known love in order to love life. This way, life becomes precious, so precious that we are able to garner just one moment deep inside the seed of eternity sown by love. By this we know that our life has been touched by grace. Then everything is different. Everything changes. Our eyes open up on a wonderful world, a promised land, a land flowing with milk and honey. Our hearts are changed. Nothing remains like it was before. This seed grows up until it becomes a giant tree, the branches of which touch the sky. A nourishing tree. The Tree of Life.

"A man can receive nothing unless it has been given to him from heaven." Wonders and treasures of heaven. I feel in my heart the unspeakable movement of grace and peace, the presence of a living love. Maybe for the first time, I touch love, which is nothing like what I could imagine. It is like a living power, moving, acting, opening the deepest doors of the soul and of the heart. My eyes open up on the true person of the One who is.

I experienced the fragility of existence. Only the truth about oneself tames this fragility and allows one to live finally with the hope of achievement and fulfillment. God takes pleasure in our fragility because we thus allow him to be.

There is an ultimate and intimate goal, one that is beyond recognition and accomplishment., which is to be happy and to fully express oneself, to be free. This is the signification.

Find out the real signification of words, words spoken out and pronounced. The meaning of life. Words of comfort. They are neither in books nor in persuasive words of human wisdom. They are deep in the heart. They come from the heart of God.

Love has not just remained an idea, an unrealistic and unachievable thought. Love became reality. We do not measure, because we are incomplete and imperfect persons. How the knowledge and understanding of this mystery would result in the transformation of our thoughts, changing our personalities to the point where everything would be new.

We have so far an intellectual or sentimental understanding of this mystery. But in truth, manifested love is of an unsearchable depth, of an infinite wealth, of a supernatural living power—an overflowing river that cleans up everything.

I would like to taste this love, to live this reality. This is what is called grace, since it has been manifested.

How to ignore, even despise, the promise made to all of abundant life, of peace and rest to the one who takes refuge under the wings of this mighty Savior. The profound joy of the one who knows that he is loved and redeemed, who knows that he is in the light of a new life, of old and forgotten things passed away!

We have received a heritage, which is the promise of abundant life, of real life, of success, peace, and happiness.

The hour has come to say yes to life, yes to happiness, yes to love, yes to abundance and prosperity, yes to grace, yes to truth, yes to freedom.

I know he is here. She is waiting for me. Without hesitation and with no haste, I am going to turn around the walls of the city (for they fall down to the sound of musical instruments) with assurance and confidence.

This the hour of the gift. This is the time of grace.

I came into a new world, a new life, a new creation. I was touched by grace. "Surely goodness and mercy shall follow me all the days of my life."

Let it be done. Do you want to take my hand? I belong to you. You are mine.

"We shall arise and build."

Time for restoration. The power of fulfillment. Being aware of self-worth. Having another identity, of a loved one, a forgiven man.

How shall we realize the beauty that dwells inside us like a light?

The truth is that he is alive. He is the living. And we are his creatures, wonderfully made. If he lives in me, then I am worthy. I do not fear. I am filled. Let the cornerstone of this new life rise up and become as strong as a thought.

Move ahead, step by step, and build, not losing what takes us so much time, effort, and price to sow, to bring up, to build.

Holding fast the twine of the truth, led by the Spirit, filled with love.

Love is the material that I work out.

I need to connect myself to that creative power, to that Source of life. I aspire to build not an intellectual edifice but a house of love. It fills me with fear, for I am so distant from this pureness—and I shall surely break it up if I reach my hand out for it myself. I am aware of my inability and am certainly afraid, at least hesitant, to desire this power for fear of the unknown, because I do not know how to do it. Such a new reality. But I confess this absolute freedom, this complete release, this true revolution. I desire the abundance of life, happiness, love, and plenitude that one receives upon entering the Promised Land, a land flowing with milk and honey.

We are followed by everything: our deeds, our thoughts, all our tried feelings. Therefore we must constantly purify those things so that the last fragrance of our lives will always be the costliest. Who will judge it? It doesn't matter. Our conscience lightens us, not like a lawyer but as a light.

Being able to listen like it is second nature, a sign of detachment and attachment. I am fulfilling my destiny even if misunderstood by men, by others. Living and existing, being myself.

About the Author

Michel Cazal was born and lives in the Indian Ocean on an island located at a cultural crossroads.

Early in his life, he would take the path of redemption and love, in a profound and intimate quest for truth and peace.

The Found Love, his first book, concentrates on true love, perfect and absolute. It reveals one of these outstanding talents of its creative author. It's refined and simple, but so intense that words of an infinite richness, like arrows with diamond tips pierce our soul and heart, take us to the borders of heavenly Eden.